First Facts™

Why in the World?

WHY Is the SOUTH POLE so COLD?

A Book about Antarctica

by Janeen R. Adil

Consultant:
Henry Brecher
Research Associate (Retired)
Byrd Polar Research Center
The Ohio State University

Capstone
press®
Mankato, Minnesota

First Facts is published by Capstone Press,
151 Good Counsel Drive, P.O. Box 669, Mankato, Minnesota 56002.
www.capstonepress.com

Library of Congress Cataloging-in-Publication Data
Adil, Janeen R.
    Why is the South Pole so cold? : a book about Antarctica / Janeen R. Adil.
    p. cm.—(First facts. Why in the world?)
    Summary: "A brief description of Antarctica, including climate, plants, animals, and exploration"—Provided by publisher.
    Includes bibliographical references and index.
    ISBN-13: 978-0-7368-6383-4 (hardcover)
    ISBN-10: 0-7368-6383-4 (hardcover)
    1. Antarctica—Juvenile literature. 2. South Pole—Juvenile literature. I. Title. II. Series.
G863.A35 2007
919.8'9—dc22   2005037721

Editorial Credits
Jennifer Besel, editor; Juliette Peters, designer; Wanda Winch, photo researcher; Scott Thoms, photo editor

Photo Credits
Corbis/Galen Rowell, 16–17; Rick Price, 10; Tim Davis, cover (penguin); Tom Van Sant, 4; Zefa/E. Hummel, 9
Getty Images Inc./Illustrated London News, 15; Time Life Pictures/Mansell, 14
Houserstock/Jan Butchofsky-Houser, 21
Minden Pictures/Frans Lanting, cover (seal), 6; Hedgehog House/Colin Monteath, 19
Shutterstock/Raymond Kasprzak, 5
Visuals Unlimited/Fritz Polking, 11
Wolfgang Kaehler, 8, 13, 20

1 2 3 4 5 6 11 10 09 08 07 06

TABLE OF CONTENTS

WHERE'S THE COLDEST PLACE ON EARTH?

The coldest place on earth lies at the very bottom of our planet. It's Antarctica, one of our seven **continents**. And right in the center of this ice-covered land is the **South Pole**.

Antarctica

SCIENTIFIC INQUIRY

Asking questions and making observations like the ones in this book are how scientists begin their research. They follow a process known as scientific inquiry.

Ask a Question

Does it get as cold in my neighborhood as it does in Antarctica?

Investigate

This winter, set up a thermometer outside where you can see it. Use a calendar to record the temperature each day. Finally, read this book to learn how cold Antarctica really is.

Explain

You note that temperatures at your house never dropped below 0 degrees Fahrenheit (minus 18 degrees Celsius). You decide that temperatures where you live don't go as low as they do in Antarctica. Record your findings in a notebook and remember to keep asking questions!

WHY IS THE SOUTH POLE SO COLD?

The South Pole is cold because sunlight only reaches the bottom of the world part of the year. Without warmth from the sun, temperatures are cold.

Thick sheets of ice cover the land in Antarctica. Some of this icy land is more than 13,000 feet (4,000 meters) above the ocean's surface. At this height, temperatures are very low.

DID YOU KNOW?
Temperatures during Antarctica's winters have dropped as low as minus 129 degrees Fahrenheit (minus 89 degrees Celsius).

Does Antarctica Have Seasons?

Antarctica does have seasons. But they are different from what we're used to. In summer, from October to March, the sun shines all the time. The air doesn't get very warm, though.

During the six months of winter, most
of the sun's rays don't reach Antarctica. The
sun may only peek above the horizon for an
hour or two. It is a very dark and cold place.

Can Animals Live in Antarctica?

Yes, but it's hard to make a home there. Layers of fat keep Weddell seals warm. The seals chew holes in the ocean ice so they can pop up for air when they need to.

Emperor penguins help each other keep warm. They huddle together to protect themselves from the wind. They take turns standing in the middle of the warm circle.

Can Plants Grow in Antarctica?

Trees can't grow in Antarctica's cold and windy weather. Shrubs and even flowers can't live there either. **Lichens** are one of only a few plants able to survive in Antarctica. These flat, tough plants grow on a rock's surface. Lichens can be black or gray, yellow or orange.

? DID YOU KNOW?
Because it is so cold in Antarctica, plants grow very slowly. Some of the plants there now may be thousands of years old.

Roald Amundsen

Has Anyone Explored Antarctica?

Many people have bravely explored this icy land. In 1911, two teams of explorers, led by Roald Amundsen and Robert Scott, raced to be the first to reach the South Pole.

Amundsen and his team, who were from Norway, beat Scott's team to the South Pole. They marked the spot with their country's flag.

Do People Live in Antarctica?

No one lives in Antarctica all the time. But many scientists and helpers do go there to work. These men and women stay in **research stations** while they study wildlife and weather. Special clothing and equipment keep them safe from the cold.

 DID YOU KNOW?
No country owns Antarctica. It belongs to everyone and is only used for research.

COULD I GO TO ANTARCTICA?

Every year, thousands of visitors go to see the wildlife and the amazing ice. Maybe someday you will too.

People in Antarctica have caused **pollution**, though. Trash and chemicals have been thrown in the ocean, hurting animals. Countries are now trying harder to keep this special land clean.

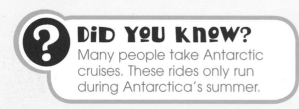

? DID YOU KNOW?
Many people take Antarctic cruises. These rides only run during Antarctica's summer.

Millions of years ago, Antarctica had a warm climate. We know this because scientists have discovered many fossils there. They've found fossils of leaves, as well as shells, shark teeth, and even dinosaurs. None of these things could live in Antarctica today.

Scientists and other workers going to Antarctica have to decide what to bring with them. Of course they need clothing, tools, food, and other supplies. For fun, they bring books, musical instruments, or games. But pets have to stay at home! What would you bring to Antarctica?

GLOSSARY

continent (KON-tuh-nuhnt)—one of earth's seven large land masses

lichen (LYE-ken)—a flat, mosslike plant that grows on trees and rocks

pollution (puh-LOO-shuhn)—materials that hurt earth's water, air, and land

research station (REE-surch STAY-shuhn)—a base or camp where scientists live, work, and study

South Pole (SOUTH POHL)—the most southern part of the earth, located at the bottom of the earth's axis; the South Pole is in Antarctica.

READ MORE

Rau, Dana Meachen. *Antarctica*. Geography of the World. Chanhassen, Minn.: Child's World, 2004.

Schaefer, A. R. *Antarctica*. The Seven Continents. Mankato, Minn.: Capstone Press, 2006.

INTERNET SITES

FactHound offers a safe, fun way to find Internet sites related to this book. All of the sites on FactHound have been researched by our staff.

Here's how:

1. Visit *www.facthound.com*

2. Choose your grade level.

3. Type in this book ID **0736863834** for age-appropriate sites. You may also browse subjects by clicking on letters, or by clicking on pictures and words.

4. Click on the **Fetch It** button.

FactHound will fetch the best sites for you!

INDEX